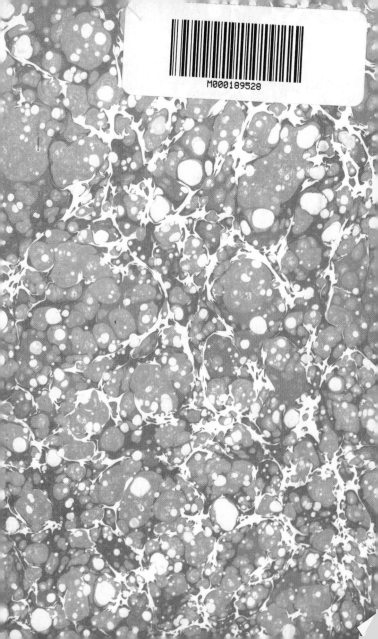

GREAT ENGLISH POETS

GREAT ENGLISH POETS

William Shakespeare

Edited and with an introduction
by Peter Porter

Clarkson N. Potter, Inc./Publishers NEW YORK
DISTRIBUTED BY CROWN PUBLISHERS, INC.

Published in the United States by Clarkson N. Potter, Inc.,
225 Park Avenue South, New York, New York 10003
and represented in Canada by the Canadian MANDA Group.
Published in Great Britain by Aurum Press Limited,
33 Museum Street, London WC1A 1LD, England

CLARKSON N. POTTER, POTTER, THE GREAT POETS,
and colophon are trademarks of Clarkson N. Potter, Inc.

Picture research by Juliet Brightmore

Manufactured in Hong Kong

Library of Congress Cataloging-in-Publication Data

Shakespeare, William, 1564–1616.
    William Shakespeare.

    (Great English Poets)
    I. Porter, Peter. II. Title. III. Series.
PR2842.P6   1987   822.3'3   87–11673
ISBN 0–517–56708–3

    10 9 8 7 6 5 4 3 2 1

    First Edition

CONTENTS

INTRODUCTION

The name of Shakespeare is probably the best known in literature, and books about him fill whole libraries. Yet the little real evidence we have about Shakespeare the man can be recorded in a few pages.

William Shakespeare was born on St George's day, 23 April 1564, in Stratford-upon-Avon, Warwickshire. His father John was a glover, with some pretension to having come down in the world. (One of William's ambitions, successfully carried out, was to apply for a coat-of-arms and so restore the Shakespeare family to the minor gentry.) The poet was educated at Stratford Grammar School, where he received a good, standard, classical training. He married Ann Hathaway, a woman somewhat older than himself, when he was only nineteen, and had three children – a daughter Susanna, and twins, a son Hamnet and another daughter Judith. His son died at the age of nine, but both girls survived to marry and have children of their own.

Shakespeare left Stratford in the mid-1580s, and there is a gap in our knowledge of his life from that point until his name as an actor and playwright begins to appear in chronicles from 1592 onwards. Thereafter, his life is the record of his plays in performance. He quickly became the most popular playwright of the day, one whose name on a playbill spelled instant success for the company performing his works. His immediately recognizable style influenced most of his fellow-playwrights, yet Shakespeare himself never emerges from the obscurity of daily life in Elizabethan and Jacobean England. Even his sonnets, which purport to tell of personal involvement with a beautiful young aristocrat and a dark lady, merely add to the confusion. We do not know when they were written and their publication was clearly not desired or intended by Shakespeare.

The great progress of his plays, which begins with either *The Comedy of Errors* or *Love's Labour's Lost* and ends twenty years later with *The Tempest* and *King Henry VIII*, fills up his London years from 1592 to 1612. All this time he was sending money home to Stratford, so that by the time he retired to his home town he had become its most eminent citizen, and lived in the largest of its private houses, New Place. He died on his birthday, in 1616, and was buried in the parish church of All Saints before the altar, under a stone marked with a doggerel verse forbidding any disturbing of his bones. In 1623 his fellow-actors, John Heminge and Henry Condell, published what came to be called the First Folio, a collection of all the plays now credited to him except for *Pericles* and *The Two Noble Kinsmen*. This well-produced and intelligently edited volume became one of the two most important books in the history of the English language. The other, also first published during the reign of King James I, was the Authorized Version of the Bible (1611).

Shakespeare is unique among the great British poets in that his poetry is predominantly in dramatic form. Other than two long poems written in a style borrowed from Italian romances, a handful of lyrics and his sonnets, all Shakespeare's verse was written to be acted in the theatre. Perhaps it was because he made his work so public that he was content to be almost invisible himself. We know far more about the life of his contemporary John Donne, for instance, than we do about that of Shakespeare, though Donne's poetry was not published until after his death. The playwright Shakespeare can touch every subject, however intense, because he is not speaking in his own person. Nothing is too painful to be divulged.

The poetry of his plays, however, lives magnificently outside its theatrical context, which makes it possible for a small book such as this to present Shakespeare as a self-sufficient poet writing separately identifiable poems. Indeed, such is the proverbial nature of Shakespeare's writing that generations of non-theatregoers have known his lines by heart and quoted them freely.

Here then is a brief quintessence of the supreme master of English. I have included some songs from the plays and ten sonnets, and I have chosen some brilliant but lesser known passages to add spice to the more famous. Shakespeare appears here as a romantic poet, forerunner of the poetical movement of Romanticism, and as an embodiment of 'the true voice of feeling'. Such an emphasis is only just, since, great playwright that he is, he is an even greater poet.

SONGS

It was a lover and his lass,
    With a hey, and a ho, and a hey nonino,
That o'er the green cornfield did pass
    In springtime, the only pretty ringtime,
When birds do sing, hey ding a ding, ding.
Sweet lovers love the spring.

Between the acres of the rye,
    With a hey, and a ho, and a hey nonino,
These pretty country folks would lie
    In springtime, &c.

This carol they began that hour,
    With a hey, and a ho, and a hey nonino,
How that a life was but a flower
    In springtime, &c.

And therefore take the present time,
    With a hey, and a ho, and a hey nonino,
For love is crownèd with the prime
    In springtime, &c.

Orpheus with his lute made trees,
And the mountain tops that freeze,
    Bow themselves when he did sing.
To his music plants and flowers
Ever sprung, as sun and showers
    There had made a lasting spring.

Every thing that heard him play,
Even the billows of the sea,
    Hung their heads, and then lay by.
In sweet music is such art,
Killing care and grief of heart
    Fall asleep, or hearing die.

What is love? 'Tis not hereafter;
Present mirth hath present laughter;
    What's to come is still unsure:
In delay there lies no plenty;
Then come kiss me, sweet and twenty,
    Youth's a stuff will not endure.

To-morrow is Saint Valentine's day.
  All in the morning betime,
And I a maid at your window,
  To be your Valentine.
Then up he rose and donned his clo'es
  And dupped the chamber door,
Let in the maid, that out a maid
  Never departed more.

By Gis and by Saint Charity,
  Alack, and fie for shame!
Young men will do't if they come to't.
  By Cock, they are to blame.
Quoth she, 'Before you tumbled me,
  You promised me to wed.'

'So would I 'a' done, by yonder sun,
  And thou hadst not come to my bed.'

When icicles hang by the wall,
    And Dick the shepherd blows his nail,
And Tom bears logs into the hall,
    And milk comes frozen home in pail,
When blood is nipped, and ways be foul,
Then nightly sings the staring owl, Tu-who;

Tu-whit, tu-who: a merry note,
While greasy Joan doth keel the pot.

When all aloud the wind doth blow,
    And coughing drowns the parson's saw,
And birds sit brooding in the snow,
    And Marian's nose looks red and raw,
When roasted crabs hiss in the bowl,
Then nightly sings the staring owl, Tu-who;

Tu-whit, tu-who: a merry note,
While greasy Joan doth keel the pot.

Blow, blow, thou winter wind,
Thou art not so unkind
    As man's ingratitude:
Thy tooth is not so keen,
Because thou art not seen,
    Although thy breath be rude.
Heigh-ho, sing heigh-ho, unto the green holly.
Most friendship is faining, most loving mere folly:
    Then, heigh-ho, the holly.
    This life is most jolly.

Freeze, freeze, thou bitter sky
That dost not bite so nigh
    As benefits forgot:
Though thou the waters warp,
Thy sting is not so sharp
    As friend rememb'red not.
Heigh-ho, sing, &c.

When that I was and a little tiny boy,
 With hey, ho, the wind and the rain,
A foolish thing was but a toy,
 For the rain it raineth every day.

But when I came to man's estate,
 With hey, ho, the wind and the rain,
'Gainst knaves and thieves men shut their gate,
 For the rain it raineth every day.

But when I came, alas, to wive,
 With hey, ho, the wind and the rain,
By swaggering could I never thrive,
 For the rain it raineth every day.

But when I came unto my beds,
 With hey, ho, the wind and the rain,
With tosspots still had drunken heads,
 For the rain it raineth every day.

A great while ago the world begun,
 With hey, ho, the wind and the rain;
But that's all one, our play is done,
 And we'll strive to please you every day.

Who is Silvia? What is she,
    That all our swains commend her?
Holy, fair, and wise is she;
    The heaven such grace did lend her,
That she might admirèd be.

Is she kind as she is fair?
    For beauty lives with kindness.
Love doth to her eyes repair,
    To help him of his blindness,
And, being helped, inhabits there.

Then to Silvia let us sing,
    That Silvia is excelling.
She excels each mortal thing
    Upon the dull earth dwelling.
To her let us garlands bring.

Come unto these yellow sands,
    And then take hands.
Curtsied when you have and kissed,
    The wild waves whist,
Foot it featly here and there;
And, sweet sprites, the burden bear.
    Hark, hark!
    Bow, wow.
    The watchdogs bark.
    Bow, wow.
    Hark, hark! I hear
    The strain of strutting chanticleer
        Cry cock-a-diddle-dow.

*   *   *   *

Full fathom five thy father lies;
    Of his bones are coral made;
Those are pearls that were his eyes;
    Nothing of him that doth fade
But doth suffer a sea-change
Into something rich and strange.
Sea nymphs hourly ring his knell:
        Ding-dong.
Hark! now I hear them – Ding-dong bell.

Fear no more the heat o' th' sun
   Nor the furious winter's rages;
Thou thy worldly task hast done,
   Home art gone and ta'en thy wages.
Golden lads and girls all must,
As chimney-sweepers, come to dust.

Fear no more the frown o' th' great;
   Thou art past the tyrant's stroke.
Care no more to clothe and eat;
   To thee the reed is as the oak.
The sceptre, learning, physic, must
All follow this and come to dust.

Fear no more the lightning flash,
   Nor th' all-dreaded thunder-stone;
Fear no slander, censure rash;
   Thou hast finished joy and moan.
All lovers young, all lovers must
Consign to thee and come to dust.

No exorciser harm thee,
Nor no witchcraft charm thee.
Ghost unlaid forbear thee;
Nothing ill come near thee.
Quiet consummation have,
And renownèd be thy grave.

Tired with all these, for restful death I cry:
As, to behold desert a beggar born,
And needy nothing trimmed in jollity,
And purest faith unhappily forsworn,
And gilded honor shamefully misplaced,
And maiden virtue rudely strumpeted,
And right perfection wrongfully disgraced,
And strength by limping sway disablèd,
And art made tongue-tied by authority,
And folly (doctor-like) controlling skill,
And simple truth miscalled simplicity,
And captive good attending captain ill.
    Tired with all these, from these would I be gone,
    Save that, to die, I leave my love alone.

When most I wink, then do mine eyes best see,
For all the day they view things unrespected;
But when I sleep, in dreams they look on thee
And, darkly bright, are bright in dark directed.
Then thou, whose shadow shadows doth make
      bright,
How would thy shadow's form form happy show
To the clear day with thy much clearer light
When to unseeing eyes thy shade shines so!
How would, I say, mine eyes be blessèd made
By looking on thee in the living day,
When in dead night thy fair imperfect shade
Through heavy sleep on sightless eyes doth stay!
    All days are nights to see till I see thee,
    And nights bright days when dreams do show
      thee me.

Not marble nor the gilded monuments
Of princes shall outlive this pow'rful rime,
But you shall shine more bright in these contents
Than unswept stone, besmeared with sluttish time.
When wasteful war shall statues overturn,
And broils root out the work of masonry,
Nor Mars his sword nor war's quick fire shall burn
The living record of your memory.
'Gainst death and all oblivious enmity
Shall you pace forth; your praise shall still find
  room
Even in the eyes of all posterity
That wear this world out to the ending doom.
 So, till the judgment that yourself arise,
  You live in this, and dwell in lovers' eyes.

Farewell: thou art too dear for my possessing,
And like enough thou know'st thy estimate.
The charter of thy worth gives thee releasing;
My bonds in thee are all determinate.
For how do I hold thee but by thy granting,
And for that riches where is my deserving?
The cause of this fair gift in me is wanting,
And so my patent back again is swerving.
Thyself thou gav'st, thy own worth then not
        knowing,
Or me, to whom thou gav'st it, else mistaking;
So thy great gift, upon misprision growing,
Comes home again, on better judgment making.
    Thus have I had thee as a dream doth flatter,
    In sleep a king, but waking no such matter.

Devouring Time, blunt thou the lion's paws,
And make the earth devour her own sweet brood;
Pluck the keen teeth from the fierce tiger's jaws,
And burn the long-lived phoenix in her blood;
Make glad and sorry seasons as thou fleet'st,
And do whate'er thou wilt, swift-footed Time,
To the wide world and all her fading sweets,
But I forbid thee one most heinous crime:
O, carve not with thy hours my love's fair brow,
Nor draw no lines there with thine antique pen;
Him in thy course untainted do allow
For beauty's pattern to succeeding men.
    Yet do thy worst, old Time: despite thy wrong,
    My love shall in my verse ever live young.

Like as the waves make towards the pebbled shore,
So do our minutes hasten to their end;
Each changing place with that which goes before,
In sequent toil all forwards do contend.
Nativity, once in the main of light,
Crawls to maturity, wherewith being crowned,
Crooked eclipses 'gainst his glory fight,
And Time that gave doth now his gift confound.
Time doth transfix the flourish set on youth
And delves the parallels in beauty's brow,
Feeds on the rarities of nature's truth,
And nothing stands but for his scythe to mow:
    And yet to times in hope my verse shall stand,
    Praising thy worth, despite his cruel hand.

Let me not to the marriage of true minds
Admit impediments; love is not love
Which alters when it alteration finds
Or bends with the remover to remove.
O, no, it is an ever-fixèd mark
That looks on tempests and is never shaken;
It is the star to every wand'ring bark,
Whose worth's unknown, although his height be
    taken.
Love's not Time's fool, though rosy lips and cheeks
Within his bending sickle's compass come;
Love alters not with his brief hours and weeks,
But bears it out even to the edge of doom.
    If this be error, and upon me proved,
    I never writ, nor no man ever loved.

They that have pow'r to hurt and will do none,
That do not do the thing they most do show,
Who, moving others, are themselves as stone,
Unmovèd, cold, and to temptation slow;
They rightly do inherit heaven's graces
And husband nature's riches from expense;
They are the lords and owners of their faces,
Others but stewards of their excellence.
The summer's flow'r is to the summer sweet,
Though to itself it only live and die;
But if that flow'r with base infection meet,
The basest weed outbraves his dignity:
    For sweetest things turn sourest by their deeds;
    Lilies that fester smell far worse than weeds.

My mistress' eyes are nothing like the sun;
Coral is far more red than her lips' red;
If snow be white, why then her breasts are dun;
If hairs be wires, black wires grow on her head.
I have seen roses damasked, red and white,
But no such roses see I in her cheeks;
And in some perfumes is there more delight
Than in the breath that from my mistress reeks.
I love to hear her speak; yet well I know
That music hath a far more pleasing sound:
I grant I never saw a goddess go;
My mistress, when she walks, treads on the ground.
   And yet, by heaven, I think my love as rare
   As any she belied with false compare.

How oft, when thou, my music, music play'st
Upon that blessèd wood whose motion sounds
With thy sweet fingers when thou gently sway'st
The wiry concord that mine ear confounds,
Do I envy those jacks that nimble leap
To kiss the tender inward of thy hand,
Whilst my poor lips, which should that harvest
     reap,
At the wood's boldness by thee blushing stand.
To be so tickled they would change their state
And situation with those dancing chips
O'er whom thy fingers walk with gentle gait,
Making dead wood more blest than living lips.
  Since saucy jacks so happy are in this,
   Give them thy fingers, me thy lips to kiss.

The Phoenix and Turtle

Let the bird of loudest lay
On the sole Arabian tree
Herald sad and trumpet be,
To whose sound chaste wings obey,

But thou shrieking harbinger,
Foul precurrer of the fiend,
Augur of the fever's end,
To this troop come thou not near.

From this session interdict
Every fowl of tyrant wing,
Save the eagle, feath'red king:
Keep the obsequy so strict.

Let the priest in surplice white,
That defunctive music can,
Be the death-divining swan,
Lest the requiem lack his right.

And thou treble-dated crow,
That thy sable gender mak'st
With the breath thou giv'st and tak'st,
'Mongst our mourners shalt thou go.

Here the anthem doth commence:
Love and constancy is dead,
Phoenix and the turtle fled
In a mutual flame from hence.

So they loved as love in twain
Had the essence but in one;
Two distincts, division none:
Number there in love was slain.

Hearts remote, yet not asunder;
Distance, and no space was seen
'Twixt this turtle and his queen;
But in them it were a wonder.

So between them love did shine
That the turtle saw his right
Flaming in the phoenix' sight:
Either was the other's mine.

Property was thus appallèd,
That the self was not the same;
Single nature's double name
Neither two nor one was callèd.

Reason, in itself confounded,
Saw division grow together,
To themselves yet either neither,
Simple were so well compounded;

That it cried, 'How true a twain
Seemeth this concordant one!
Love hath reason, reason none,
If what parts can so remain.'

Whereupon it made this threne
To the phoenix and the dove,
Co-supremes and stars of love,
As chorus to their tragic scene.

THRENOS

Beauty, truth, and rarity,
Grace in all simplicity,
Here enclosed, in cinders lie.

Death is now the phoenix' nest;
And the turtle's loyal breast
To eternity doth rest,

Leaving no posterity:
'Twas not their infirmity,
It was married chastity.

Truth may seem, but cannot be;
Beauty brag, but 'tis not she:
Truth and Beauty buried be.

To this urn let those repair
That are either true or fair;
For these dead birds sigh a prayer.

VERSE FROM THE PLAYS

Othello

Jealous Othello watches Desdemona as she sleeps
It is the cause, it is the cause, my soul.
Let me not name it to you, you chaste stars!
It is the cause. Yet I'll not shed her blood,
Not scar that whiter skin of hers than snow,
And smooth as monumental alabaster.
Yet she must die, else she'll betray more men.
Put out the light, and then put out the light.
If I quench thee, thou flaming minister,
I can again thy former light restore,
Should I repent me; but once put out thy light,
Thou cunning'st pattern of excelling nature,
I know not where is that Promethean heat
That can thy light relume. When I have plucked
    the rose,
I cannot give it vital growth again;
It needs must wither. I'll smell thee on the tree.
O balmy breath, that dost almost persuade
Justice to break her sword! One more, one more!
Be thus when thou art dead, and I will kill thee,
And love thee after. One more, and that's the last!
So sweet was ne'er so fatal. I must weep,
But they are cruel tears. This sorrow's heavenly;
It strikes where it doth love. She wakes.

Troilus and Cressida

The ardent lover Troilus anticipates his love
I am giddy; expectation whirls me round.
Th' imaginary relish is so sweet
That it enchants my sense. What will it be
When that the wat'ry palates taste indeed
Love's thrice-repurèd nectar? Death, I fear me,
Sounding destruction, or some joy too fine,
Too subtle, potent, tuned too sharp in sweetness
For the capacity of my ruder powers.

Two Gentlemen of Verona

Proteus tells of the power of poetry in the voice of a lover
Say that upon the altar of her beauty
You sacrifice your tears, your sighs, your heart.
Write till your ink be dry, and with your tears
Moist it again, and frame some feeling line
That may discover such integrity.
For Orpheus' lute was strung with poets' sinews,
Whose golden touch could soften steel and stones,
Make tigers tame, and huge leviathans
Forsake unsounded deeps to dance on sands.
After your dire-lamenting elegies,
Visit by night your lady's chamber window
With some sweet consort. To their instruments
Tune a deploring dump; the night's dead silence
Will well become such sweet-complaining
        grievance.
This, or else nothing, will inherit her.

Antony and Cleopatra

Antony's first meeting with Cleopatra
The barge she sat in, like a burnished throne,
Burned on the water: the poop was beaten gold;
Purple the sails, and so perfumed that
The winds were lovesick with them; the oars were silver,
Which to the tune of flutes kept stroke, and made
The water which they beat to follow faster,
As amorous of their strokes. For her own person,
It beggared all description: she did lie
In her pavilion, cloth-of-gold of tissue,
O'erpicturing that Venus where we see
The fancy outwork nature. On each side her
Stood pretty dimpled boys, like smiling Cupids,
With divers-colored fans, whose wind did seem
To glow the delicate cheeks which they did cool,
And what they undid did. . . .
Her gentlewomen, like the Nereides,
So many mermaids, tended her i' th' eyes,
And made their bends adornings. At the helm
A seeming mermaid steers: the silken tackle
Swell with the touches of those flower-soft hands,
That yarely frame the office. From the barge
A strange invisible perfume hits the sense
Of the adjacent wharfs. The city cast
Her people out upon her; and Antony,
Enthroned i' th' market place, did sit alone,
Whistling to th' air; which, but for vacancy,
Had gone to gaze on Cleopatra too,
And made a gap in nature.

A Midsummer Night's Dream

Oberon sends Puck to find the flower of love
I know a bank where the wild thyme blows,
Where oxlips and the nodding violet grows,
Quite over-canopied with luscious woodbine,
With sweet musk-roses, and with eglantine.
There sleeps Titania sometime of the night,
Lulled in these flowers with dances and delight;
And there the snake throws her enamelled skin,
Weed wide enough to wrap a fairy in.
And with the juice of this I'll streak her eyes
And make her full of hateful fantasies.

Titania exhorts her fairies to attend on Bottom
Be kind and courteous to this gentleman.
Hop in his walks and gambol in his eyes;
Feed him with apricocks and dewberries,
With purple grapes, green figs, and mulberries;
The honey-bags steal from the humblebees,
And for night tapers crop their waxen thighs,
And light them at the fiery glowworm's eyes,
To have my love to bed and to arise;
And pluck the wings from painted butterflies
To fan the moonbeams from his sleeping eyes.
Nod to him, elves, and do him courtesies.

The fairies bless the lovers in Duke Theseus's palace

PUCK

Now the hungry lion roars,
    And the wolf behowls the moon;

Whilst the heavy ploughman snores,
    All with weary task fordone.
Now the wasted brands do glow,
    Whilst the screech owl, screeching loud,
Puts the wretch that lies in woe
    In remembrance of a shroud.
Now it is the time of night
    That the graves, all gaping wide,
Every one lets forth his sprite,
    In the churchway paths to glide.
And we fairies, that do run
    By the triple Hecate's team
From the presence of the sun,
    Following darkness like a dream,
Now are frolic. Not a mouse
Shall disturb this hallowed house.
I am sent, with broom, before,
To sweep the dust behind the door.

OBERON

Through the house give glimmering light,
    By the dead and drowsy fire;
Every elf and fairy sprite
    Hop as light as bird from brier;
And this ditty, after me,
Sing, and dance it trippingly.

TITANIA
First rehearse your song by rote,
To each word a warbling note.
Hand in hand, with fairy grace,
Will we sing, and bless this place.

Hamlet

Hamlet soliloquizes on his mother's perfidy
O that this too too solid flesh would melt,
Thaw, and resolve itself into a dew,
Or that the Everlasting had not fixed
His canon 'gainst self-slaughter. O God, God,
How weary, stale, flat, and unprofitable
Seem to me all the uses of this world!
Fie on't, ah, fie, 'tis an unweeded garden
That grows to seed. Things rank and gross in nature
Possess it merely. That it should come to this,
But two months dead, nay, not so much, not two,
So excellent a king, that was to this
Hyperion to a satyr, so loving to my mother
That he might not beteem the winds of heaven
Visit her face too roughly. Heaven and earth,
Must I remember? Why, she would hang on him
As if increase of appetite had grown
By what it fed on, and yet within a month–
Let me not think on't; frailty, thy name is woman–
A little month, or ere those shoes were old
With which she followed my poor father's body
Like Niobe, all tears, why she, even she–
O God, a beast that wants discourse of reason

Would have mourned longer – married with my
      uncle,
My father's brother, but no more like my father
Than I to Hercules. Within a month,
Ere yet the salt of most unrighteous tears
Had left the flushing in her gallèd eyes,
She married. O, most wicked speed, to post
With such dexterity to incestuous sheets!
It is not nor it cannot come to good.
But break my heart, for I must hold my tongue.

Queen Gertrude relates how Ophelia died
There is a willow grows askant the brook,
That shows his hoar leaves in the glassy stream.
Therewith fantastic garlands did she make
Of crowflowers, nettles, daisies, and long purples,
That liberal shepherds give a grosser name,
But our cold maids do dead men's fingers call them.
There on the pendent boughs her crownet weeds
Clamb'ring to hang, an envious sliver broke,
When down her weedy trophies and herself
Fell in the weeping brook. Her clothes spread wide,
And mermaid-like a while they bore her up,
Which time she chanted snatches of old lauds,
As one incapable of her own distress,
Or like a creature native and indued
Unto that element. But long it could not be
Till that her garments, heavy with their drink,
Pulled the poor wretch from her melodious lay
To muddy death.

Macbeth

Macbeth responds to the news of Lady Macbeth's death
To-morrow, and to-morrow, and to-morrow
Creeps in this petty pace from day to day
To the last syllable of recorded time,
And all our yesterdays have lighted fools
The way to dusty death. Out, out, brief candle!
Life's but a walking shadow, a poor player
That struts and frets his hour upon the stage
And then is heard no more. It is a tale
Told by an idiot, full of sound and fury,
Signifying nothing.

The Merchant of Venice

Lorenzo tells Jessica of the power of music
How sweet the moonlight sleeps upon this bank!
Here will we sit and let the sounds of music
Creep in our ears; soft stillness and the night
Become the touches of sweet harmony.
Sit, Jessica. Look how the floor of heaven
Is thick inlaid with patens of bright gold.
There's not the smallest orb which thou behold'st
But in his motion like an angel sings,
Still quiring to the young-eyed cherubins;
Such harmony is in immortal souls,

But whilst this muddy vesture of decay
Doth grossly close it in, we cannot hear it.
Come ho, and wake Diana with a hymn!
With sweetest touches pierce your mistress' ear
And draw her home with music. . . .
For do but note a wild and wanton herd
Or race of youthful and unhandled colts
Fetching mad bounds, bellowing and neighing
      loud,
Which is the hot condition of their blood:
If they but hear perchance a trumpet sound,
Or any air of music touch their ears,
You shall perceive them make a mutual stand,
Their savage eyes turned to a modest gaze
By the sweet power of music. Therefore the poet
Did feign that Orpheus drew trees, stones, and
      floods;
Since naught so stockish, hard, and full of rage
But music for the time doth change his nature.
The man that hath no music in himself,
Nor is not moved with concord of sweet sounds,
Is fit for treasons, stratagems, and spoils;
The motions of his spirit are dull as night,
And his affections dark as Erebus.
Let no such man be trusted.

Twelfth Night

Duke Orsino and Viola (disguised as a man)
discuss the effects of love

DUKE

There is no woman's sides
Can bide the beating of so strong a passion
As love doth give my heart; no woman's heart
So big to hold so much; they lack retention.
Alas, their love may be called appetite,
No motion of the liver but the palate,
That suffers surfeit, cloyment, and revolt;
But mine is all as hungry as the sea
And can digest as much. Make no compare
Between that love a woman can bear me
And that I owe Olivia. . . .

VIOLA

She never told her love,
But let concealment, like a worm i' th' bud,
Feed on her damask cheek. She pined in thought;
And, with a green and yellow melancholy,
She sat like Patience on a monument,
Smiling at grief. Was not this love indeed?
We men may say more, swear more; but indeed
Our shows are more than will; for still we prove
Much in our vows but little in our love.

King Richard II

The dying John of Gaunt addresses his native land
This royal throne of kings, this scept'red isle,
This earth of majesty, this seat of Mars,
This other Eden, demi-paradise,
This fortress built by Nature for herself
Against infection and the hand of war,
This happy breed of men, this little world,
This precious stone set in the silver sea,
Which serves it in the office of a wall,
Or as a moat defensive to a house,
Against the envy of less happier lands;
This blessed plot, this earth, this realm, this
     England,
This nurse, this teeming womb of royal kings,
Feared by their breed and famous by their birth,
Renownèd for their deeds as far from home,
For Christian service and true chivalry,
As is the sepulchre in stubborn Jewry
Of the world's ransom, blessed Mary's son;
This land of such dear souls, this dear dear land,
Dear for her reputation through the world,
Is now leased out (I die pronouncing it)
Like to a tenement or pelting farm.
England, bound in with the triumphant sea,
Whose rocky shore beats back the envious siege
Of wat'ry Neptune, is now bound in with shame,
With inky blots and rotten parchment bonds.
That England that was wont to conquer others
Hath made a shameful conquest of itself.

The Tempest

The monster Caliban is touched by music
Be not afeard: the isle is full of noises,
Sounds and sweet airs that give delight and hurt not.
Sometimes a thousand twangling instruments
Will hum about mine ears; and sometime voices
That, if I then had waked after long sleep,
Will make me sleep again; and then, in dreaming,
The clouds methought would open and show riches
Ready to drop upon me, that, when I waked,
I cried to dream again.

Prospero bids farewell to the spirits
Our revels now are ended. These our actors,
As I foretold you, were all spirits and
Are melted into air, into thin air;
And, like the baseless fabric of this vision,
The cloud-capped tow'rs, the gorgeous palaces,
The solemn temples, the great globe itself,
Yea, all which it inherit, shall dissolve,
And, like this insubstantial pageant faded,
Leave not a rack behind. We are such stuff
As dreams are made on, and our little life
Is rounded with a sleep.

Prospero renounces his art as magician
Ye elves of hills, brooks, standing lakes, and
      groves,
And ye that on the sands with printless foot
Do chase the ebbing Neptune, and do fly him
When he comes back; you demi-puppets that
By moonshine do the green sour ringlets make,
Whereof the ewe not bites; and you whose pastime
Is to make midnight mushrumps, that rejoice
To hear the solemn curfew; by whose aid
(Weak masters though ye be) I have bedimmed
The noontide sun, called forth the mutinous
      winds,
And 'twixt the green sea and the azured vault
Set roaring war; to the dread rattling thunder
Have I given fire and rifted Jove's stout oak
With his own bolt; the strong-based promontory
Have I made shake and by the spurs plucked up
The pine and cedar; graves at my command
Have waked their sleepers, oped, and let 'em forth
By my so potent art. But this rough magic
I here abjure; and when I have required
Some heavenly music (which even now I do)
To work mine end upon their senses that
This airy charm is for, I'll break my staff,
Bury it certain fathoms in the earth,
And deeper than did ever plummet sound
I'll drown my book.

NOTES ON THE POEMS

The songs on pages 14–25 are from the following plays:
p.14 *Love's Labour's Lost* Act V scene iii; **p.16** *King Henry VIII* Act III scene i; *Twelfth Night* Act II scene iii; **p.17** *Hamlet* Act IV scene v; **p.18** *Love's Labour's Lost* Act V scene ii; **p.20** *As You Like It* Act II scene vii; **p.21** *Twelfth Night* Act V scene i; **p.22** *Two Gentlemen of Verona* Act IV scene ii; **p.24** *The Tempest* Act I scene ii; **p.25** *Cymbeline* Act IV scene iii.

The numbers of the sonnets on pages 26–38 are as follows:
p.26 no. 66; **p.28** no. 43; **p.29** no. 55; **p.30** no. 87; **p.32** no. 19; **p.33** no. 60; **p.35** no. 116; **p.36** no. 94; **p.37** no. 130; **p.38** no. 128.

The verse on pages 43–59 is from the following plays:
p.43 *Othello* Act V scene ii; **p.44** *Troilus and Cressida* Act III scene ii; *Two Gentlemen of Verona* Act III scene ii; **p.45** *Antony and Cleopatra* Act II scene ii; **p.46** *A Midsummer Night's Dream* Act II scene i; Act III scene 1; **pp. 48–9** *A Midsummer Night's Dream* Act V scene 1; **pp. 49-50** *Hamlet* Act I scene ii; **p.50** *Hamlet* Act IV scene vii; **p.52** *Macbeth* Act I scene vi; **pp. 52–3** *The Merchant of Venice* Act V scene i; **p.55** *Twelfth Night* Act II scene iv; **p.56** *King Richard II* Act II scene i; **p.57** *The Tempest* Act III scene ii; Act IV scene i; **p.59** *The Tempest* Act V scene i.

NOTES ON THE PICTURES

p.6   A representation of the month of May from the calendar of an early sixteenth-century Flemish book of hours by Simon Benninck (1483/4–1561). Victoria and Albert Museum, London. Crown Copyright.

p.15   August, from a book of hours by Simon Benninck. Victoria and Albert Museum, London. Crown Copyright.

p.19   Detail of February from the *Très Riches Heures* of Jean, duc de Berry, by the Limbourg brothers, early fifteenth century. Musée Condé, Chantilly. Photo: Giraudon, Paris.

p.23   Miniature portrait of a lady called Frances, Countess of

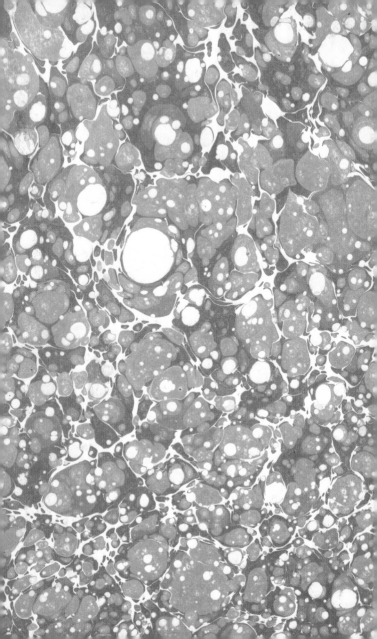